SMART BRAIN RIGHT BRAIN

An Introduction to Aerospace Engineering

Om KIDZ
An imprint of Om Books International

Om Kidz | Om Books International

Reprinted in 2023

Corporate & Editorial Office
A-12, Sector 64, Noida 201 301
Uttar Pradesh, India
Phone: +91 120 477 4100
Email: editorial@ombooks.com
Website: www.ombooksinternational.com

Sales Office
107, Ansari Road, Darya Ganj
New Delhi 110 002, India
Phone: +91 11 4000 9000
Email: sales@ombooks.com

Author: Shweta Sinha
Editor: Kirti Pathak
Art & Design: Anshuman Pandey, Gaurav Bhandari, Harish Arya

ISBN: 978-93-52768-47-9

Printed in India

10 9 8 7 6 5 4 3 2

CONTENTS

1. Up, Up and Away

Tim loves to play with toy planes. His room is full of them.

That's not surprising. Afterall, Tim's mom is an aerospace engineer. She designs and builds aircrafts and other things that can fly. Tim's dad is a pilot. He flies the aircrafts that engineers like Tim's mom work on.

POCKET FACT

An astronaut is a person who is specially trained to fly into outer space.

Aerospace engineers work in two main areas – astronautical and aeronautical.

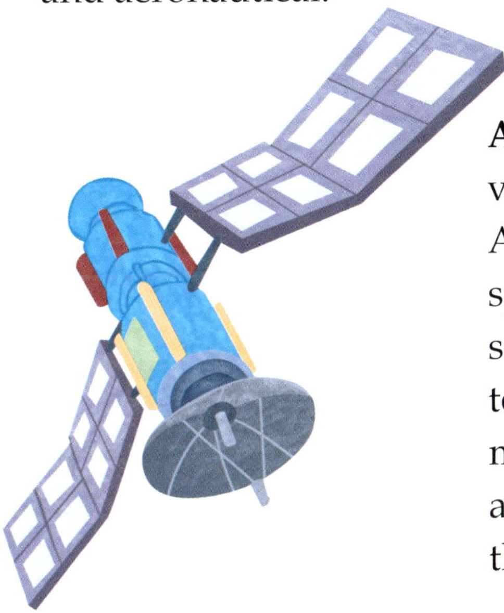

Astronautical engineers build vehicles that fly into outer space. A lot of the vehicles for outer space have been created to carry satellites. Satellites are needed to make television broadcasts, to monitor the weather and climate, and even to link computers on the internet.

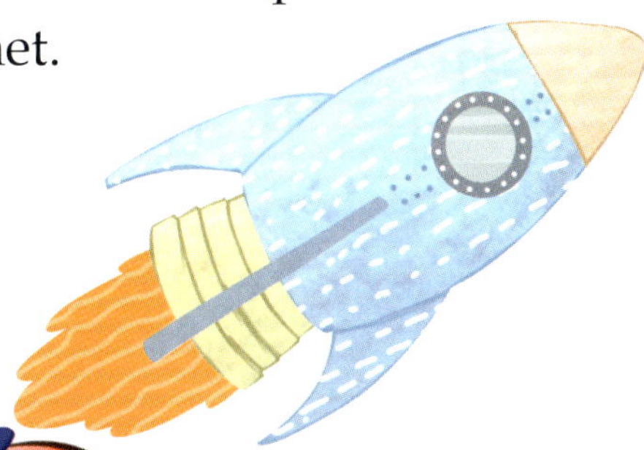

Aeronautical engineers work on machines that fly inside the Earth's atmosphere. This includes aeroplanes, jets, helicopters, drones, etc.

DID YOU KNOW?

Some aircrafts do not have a human pilot flying them. Such aircrafts are called unmanned aerial vehicles (UAV).

2. History of Flight

The first time people started flying was in a hot air balloon. In 1783, brothers Joseph and Étienne Montgolfier launched the first balloon in air with people on board. The idea of a hot air balloon first came to them as they watched smoke from a fire force a silk bag to float in the air.

When air is heated, it expands and becomes lighter.

The heated air trapped inside the balloon is lighter than the cooler air outside. The balloon full of heated air begins to rise up.

POCKET FACT

A hot air balloon falls back to the ground when the air inside it cools down.

Airships

The early balloons simply drifted with the wind. This meant, you could not control where the balloon went. You might want to reach school, but could end up in the city hall.

The invention of airships made balloons steerable. Airships were elongated balloons filled with hydrogen, a gas that was lighter than air. They had propellers to drive them forward. A rudder was used to control the direction of travel.

Today, airships are used for advertising. Known as blimps, they float in air, displaying company names or slogans on their sides.

DID YOU KNOW?

Airships were some of the largest aircrafts to fly in our skies.

Gliders

A glider was the first aircraft with wings. It has no power of its own and relies on wind power to glide in the air.

George Cayley, a British engineer, built the world's first glider in 1853. Cayley's glider made a short flight before crash landing.

Otto Lilienthal of Germany continued to work on the glider design. He built a series of gliders that he flew by jumping into the wind from high places.

DID YOU KNOW?

Otto Lilienthal had built a hill of his own to test the gliders he designed.

The Wright Flyer

Otto Lilienthal inspired many others to take up flying. Amongst them were Wilbur and Orville Wright, two bicycle makers from the USA. The Wright brothers experimented with gliders at first. It taught them how to control an aircraft in air.

Soon, they built their own aircraft, which they named the 'Flyer'. To power the Flyer, the brothers built a small and light gasoline engine. Orville successfully flew the Flyer in 1903.

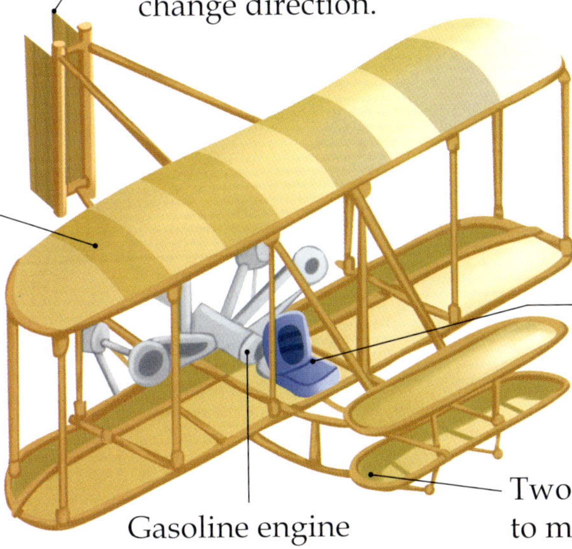

POCKET FACT

The first powered flight by Orville Wright was just a short hop and lasted only 12 seconds.

Modern Aircrafts

The first time Orville Wright flew the Flyer, the aircraft rose just nine feet. That is about as high as your bedroom's ceiling. Modern aeroplanes can now fly higher than the tallest mountain on Earth.

The first aircrafts were used during World War I as bombers and for spying on enemy grounds. Most of the early aircrafts were made of wood and fabric, much like the Wright Flyer.

DID YOU KNOW?

KLM Royal Dutch Airlines is the world's oldest airline company, established in 1919.

The Jet Age

By the 1930s, engineers began designing aircrafts made entirely of metal. The invention of the jet engine allowed aeroplanes to fly much faster than before. They also began travelling greater distances.

The **Douglas DC-2** was a powerful aircraft that could fly across the Unites States, from New York to Los Angeles. It was introduced in 1934.

As more and more people started to travel by air, aerospace engineers needed to build bigger planes. 'Jumbo Jet' was the nickname given to the first large-sized aircraft, the Beoing 747, that came into service in 1970.

POCKET FACT

In 1970, the Jumbo Jet flew more than 350 people from New York to London across the Atlantic ocean.

Faster than Sound

Aerospace engineers have always looked for ways to make aircrafts fly faster and faster. The Concorde was the fastest aeroplane ever built. It was so fast, it could cross the Atlantic ocean in only 3.5 hours. An ordinary aeroplane takes nearly eight hours for the same journey.

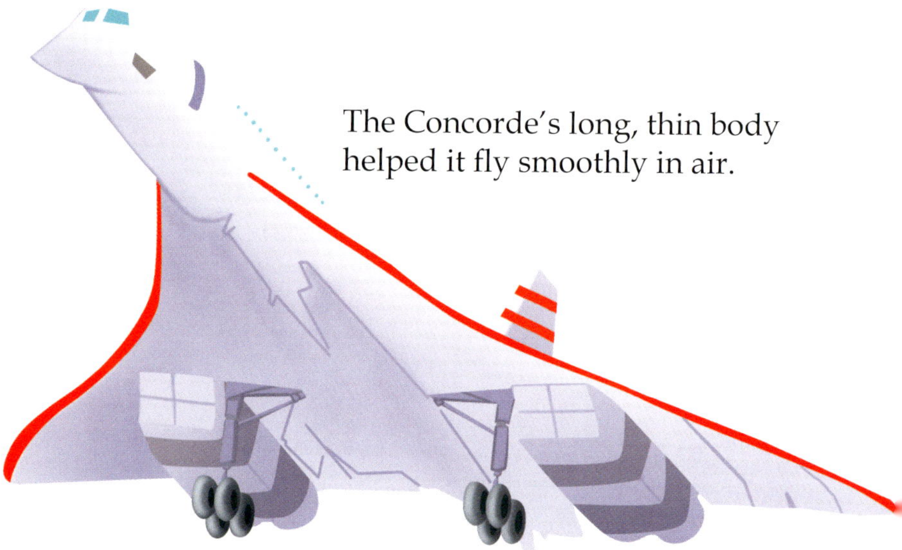

The Concorde's long, thin body helped it fly smoothly in air.

A Concorde had four engines. They burnt twice as much fuel as an ordinary aeroplane.

The Concorde was a supersonic aeroplane. It could travel faster than sound.

POCKET FACT

Many airports had banned the Concorde as it made a lot of noise.

3. Flying High

Aeroplanes

An aeroplane is an aircraft with fixed wings.

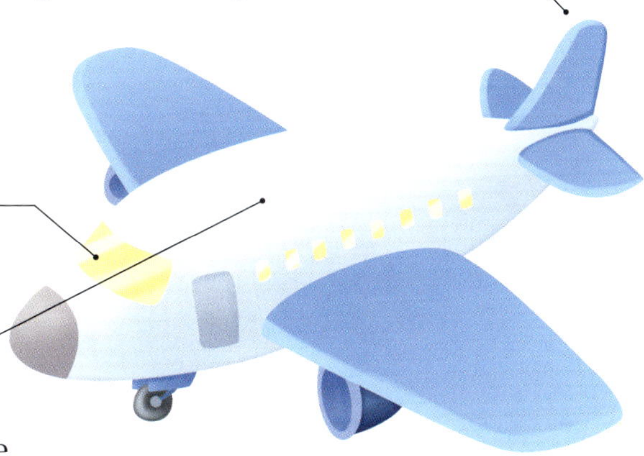

The aeroplane's engine lies inside the fuselage. The engine gives the aeroplane the force to move forward.

DID YOU KNOW? Gliders are also fixed-wing aircrafts, but do not have any engines.

Airliners

Today anyone can fly in an aeroplane by buying a ticket. Airline services for passengers started around 1918. Airliners fly on fixed routes between cities.

Cargo Planes

Some planes don't carry passengers. They are made only to carry goods and cargo around the world.

POCKET FACT

Charles Furnas was the first airline passenger who flew with the Wright brothers on one of their machines in 1908.

Seaplanes

Planes that can take off and land on water instead of land are called seaplanes.

Floats allow the seaplane to take-off and land on water.

Military Aircrafts

Aeroplanes have been used by the military since World War I. Today's jet fighters are an important part of modern warfare. They are used to transport troops, rescue the injured and attack enemy forces with bombs and machine guns.

Weapons

DID YOU KNOW? The Lockheed SR-71, also known as the Blackbird, was the fastest jet ever. It was a spy plane owned by the US military.

Helicopters

Unlike an aeroplane, which has wings that do not move, a helicopter has a set of spinning rotor blades on top. A helicopter can fly straight up from the ground. It can fly in both forward and backward directions. Helicopters can also hover in the same spot while in air.

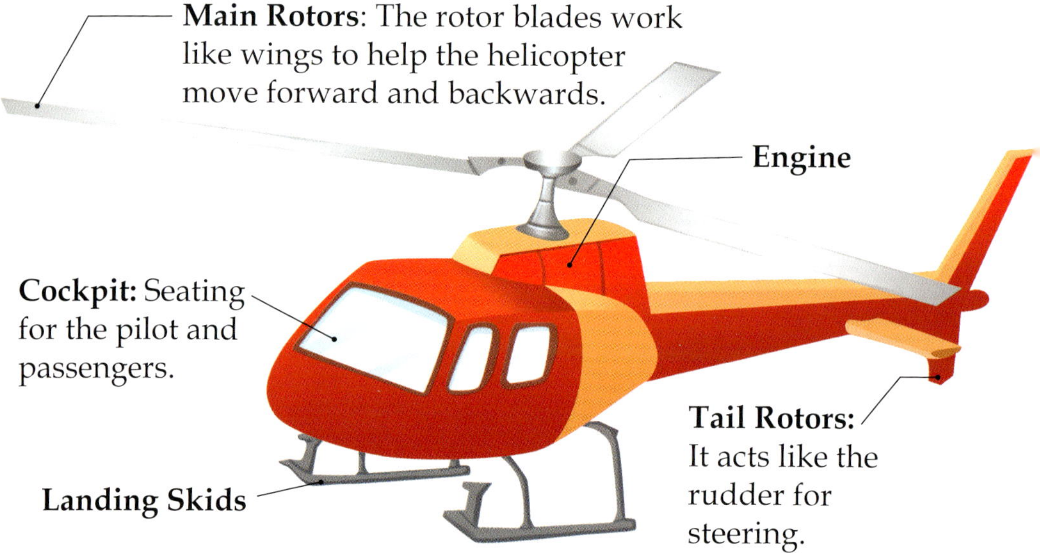

One of the main uses of a helicopter is to rescue people from places that are hard to reach. This includes mountain tops and the middle of an ocean.

POCKET FACT

Helicopters are also called helos, whirlybirds, choppers and copters.

Drones

A drone is an unmanned aerial vehicle (UAV). Drones can be as big as an aeroplane or small enough to fit in your palm.

A drone has no human pilot onboard. You can fly a drone using a remote control device. Sometimes a drone is flown by a computer installed on the drone itself. Essentially, a drone is a flying robot.

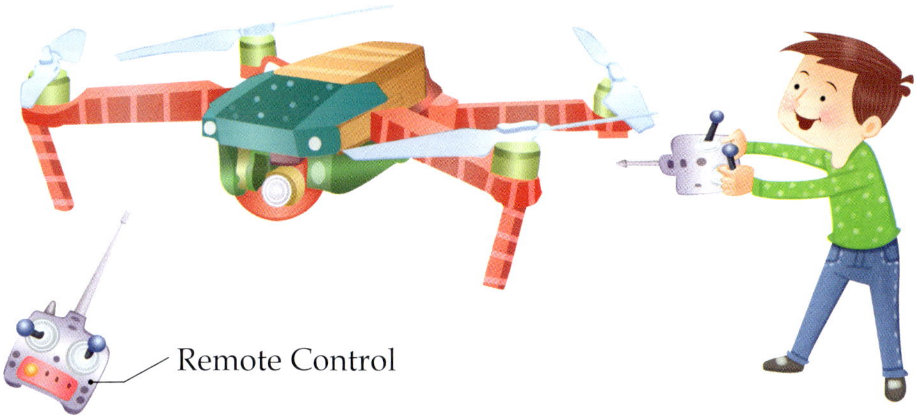

Drones were originally used by the military to spy on their enemy. Now drones are used for many more things. Photographers use them to take aerial shots and make videos. Firefighters use them to assess fire, and for search and rescue. Farmers use drones to check on their crops.

DID YOU KNOW?

Before drones came to be used, photographers flew cameras on kites to capture shots from the air.

4. How Does an Aeroplane Fly?

An aeroplane is pulled and pushed by four forces that help it fly.

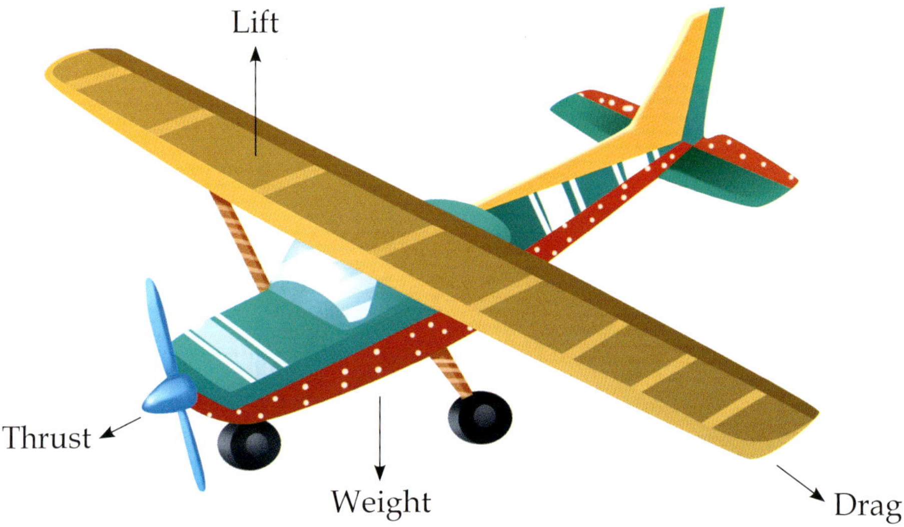

Lift helps the plane rise in the air and stay there. Wind flows both over and under the wings of an aeroplane. The wings push the air downwards. In return, air pushes the wings upwards. This force is called the 'lift'.

Try this:

Fill a bucket with water. Now take a table tennis paddle and hold it horizontally under water. Tilt the paddle a little upwards in the front and move it along. You can feel the paddle trying to rise upward in water. This the same effect that air has on an aeroplane's wings.

Thrust moves the plane forward. The engine produces the thrust. In a jet engine, air is first sucked into a small space in the front. Inside, it is sprayed with fuel and set on fire. The mixture of air and fuel shoots out from the back of the engine, pushing the aeroplane forward.

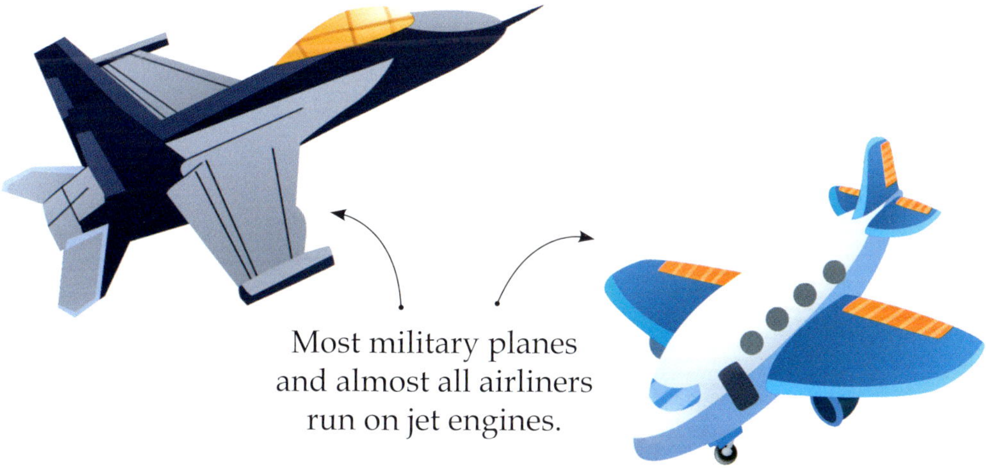

Most military planes and almost all airliners run on jet engines.

Weight is the force with which the Earth pulls the aeroplane to the ground. The weight of an aeroplane is spread evenly from front to back. It keeps the plane balanced.

Drag is the air resistance that slows down the plane. You too can feel drag when you walk against a strong wind.

And, of course, in addition to these four forces, an aeroplane needs a pilot to fly it!

POCKET FACT

The shape of an aeroplane's wings allows wind to travel faster on the top and slower at the bottom.

5. Feats in Flying

Ever since the Wright brothers invented the aeroplane, pilots have undertaken some great journeys around the world. One of the biggest challenges at the beginning was making a long flight. Louis Blériot was the first person to fly across the English Channel on a powered aircraft in 1909.

In 1919, John Alcock and Arthur Brown flew non-stop across the Atlantic ocean. Only a few years later, Charles Lindbergh flew across the Atlantic on his own in 1927.

DID YOU KNOW? In 1933, Wiley Post flew solo across the world. His journey took almost eight days to complete.

Amazing Amelia Earhart

In 1928, Amelia Earhart became the first woman to fly across the Atlantic. But Amelia dreamed of doing what Charles Lindbergh had done. She wanted to cross the ocean solo. On 20 May 1932, she took off from Newfoundland, Canada, in her bright red aeroplane. Her journey was not easy. She had to fight bad weather and thick clouds before successfully landing in Ireland. Amelia became only the second person to fly solo across the ocean. Later, she also became the first person to cross both the Atlantic and the Pacific oceans.

POCKET FACT

Amelia Earhart mysteriously disappeared while flying over the Pacific ocean in 1937. She was never found.

6. Rocket Science

A spacecraft is a vehicle that travels into space. Some spacecrafts stay close to the Earth and go around it in circles. This is called orbiting. The Moon orbits the Earth and the Earth itself orbits the Sun.

Most of the spacecrafts in orbit are satellites. Satellites are used for different jobs including communications, GPS, weather forecasting and more.

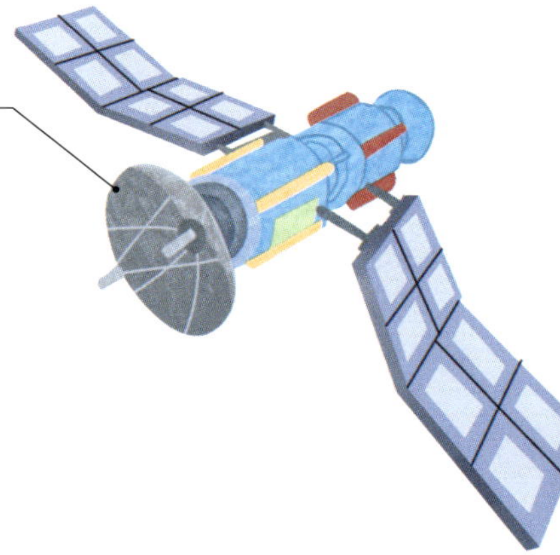

The International Space Station is a large spacecraft orbiting the Earth. Astronauts from different countries live here.

POCKET FACT

The "wings" on a spacecraft are actually solar panels. They turn sunlight into power for the spacecraft to work.

Sometimes a spacecraft is sent far away to explore other space objects. So far humans have only landed on the moon. All spacecrafts sent to other planets have been unmanned.

The Apollo spacecrafts were designed to carry people to the moon and bring them back.

Probes are spacecrafts without any crew onboard. They can fly for millions of miles. Their job is to collect pictures and information and send them back to scientists on Earth.

DID YOU KNOW? The most visited planet has been Mars. Several wheeled probes have landed on the planet.

Lift Off

Spacecrafts are launched into space by rockets. During World War II, the Germans built a rocket, V2. It was designed to attack far-off enemy cities. After the war was over, scientists figured they could use the technology to go into space.

Unlike an aeroplane, a rocket is not flown by the crew inside it. Onboard computers run the launch, monitored by the people on Earth at mission control.

DID YOU KNOW?

The first person to go into space was a Russian cosmonaut, Yuri Gagarin, in 1961.

Getting Home

So how do astronauts return to Earth from space?

To leave its orbit, the spacecraft has to slow down by firing up its rocket.

The fuel tanks, engine and all parts other than the crew cabin separate and fall off.

The crew cabin enters the Earth's atmosphere at great speed. This makes it very hot. It looks like a shooting star from the ground.

A heat shield prevents the cabin from burning up. A parachute slows it down so the cabin can land softly.

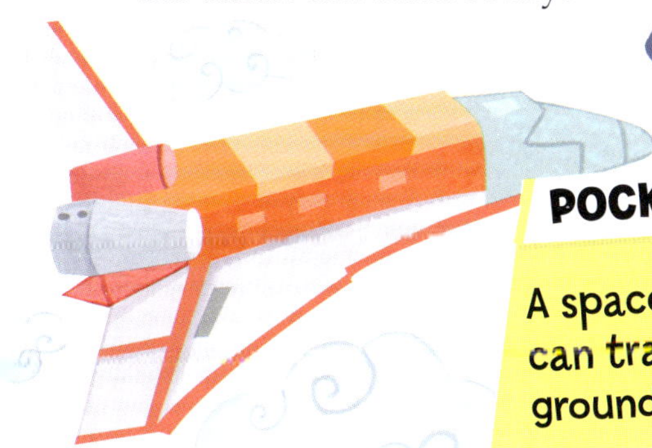

POCKET FACT

A space plane is a spacecraft that can travel to space and come back to ground again like an aeroplane.

7. Activity: Make a Parachute

A parachute is an umbrella-shaped device you can use to float down slowly and safely from a height. Pilots, soldiers and aviation enthusiasts use parachutes to safely jump to the ground from aeroplanes. While using a real parachute requires practice, we can make a small parachute for fun.

You need:

- Disposable paper cup
- Plastic bag
- String
- Paper Punch
- Scissors
- Ruler or tape measure

Step 1. Punch holes just under the rim of the cup. Punch four holes that are equal distance apart.	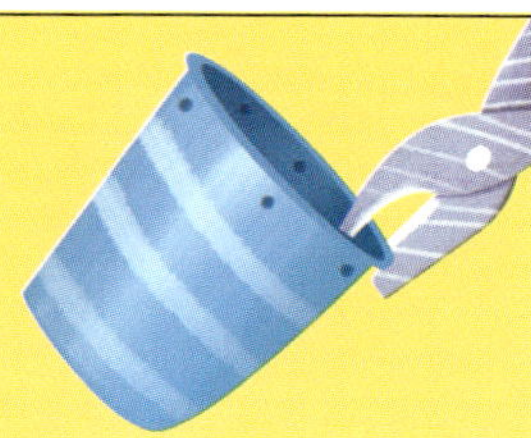
Step 2. Cut up the plastic bag into a 14-inch square.	

Step 3. Cut four 14-inch lengths of string. Tie them to the corners of the plastic square.

Step 4. Tie each string to a different hole in the cup. Your parachute is ready.

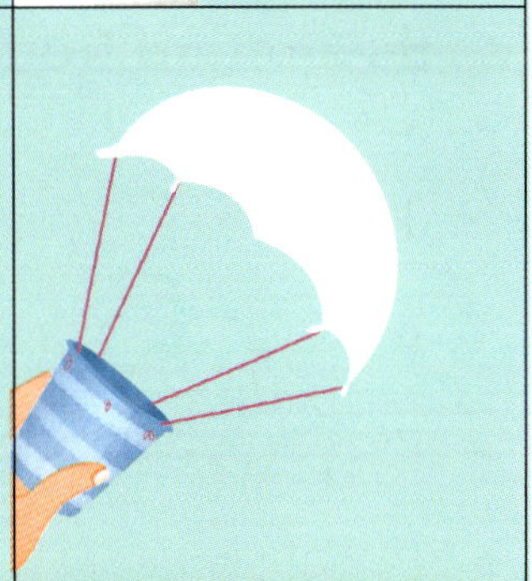

Step 5. Drop the parachute from a high place, like the landing deck of the slide in the playground. Watch the parachute slowly fall to ground.

How does a parachute work?

As the parachute falls, it fans out fully. Air that gets under the parachute slows down the fall. This is known as air resistance or drag. Thus, the cup glides down gracefully under the parachute.

Let's Get Active

Who am I?

Guess the person's name to match each statement.

1. "We invented the hot air balloon in 1783."

   (a) Warner Brothers (b) Kennedy Brothers
   (c) Wright Brothers (d) Montgolfier Brothers

2. "I built the first glider, but my glider crashed after a short flight."

   (a) George Mountbatten (b) George Cayley
   (c) George Little (d) George Washington

3. "I was the first person to successfully fly an aeroplane that I built with my brother."

   (a) Orville Wright (b) Wilbur Wright
   (c) Otto Lilienthal (d) Joseph Montgolfier

4. "Flying was my childhood dream and I became the first woman to fly across the Atlantic Ocean."

   (a) Bessie Coleman (b) Jacqueline Cochran
   (c) Amelia Earhart (d) Harriet Quimby

5. "I am a Soviet cosmonaut. I was the first person to go into space."

   (a) Neil Armstrong (b) Yuri Gagarin
   (c) Laika (d) Valentina Tereshkova

Unscramble the words to get the correct answer:

1. Air _____ when it is heated and becomes lighter.

SDEANPX

2. Airships used for advertising are called ________.

SMLBIP

3. A ______ was the first aircraft with wings.

IRELGD

4. The pilot sits in the ________ of an aeroplane.

ITCCOKP

5. A helicopter has _______ blades instead of wings.

TOORR

True or False

1. A drone can be so small that it can fit in your palm. (True/False)
2. Aerospace engineers are specially trained to fly into outer space. (True/False)
3. The force that helps an aeroplane rise up in air is thrust. (True/False)
4. A helicopter can move forward, backward and also hover in air. (True/False)
5. Jumbo Jet is a nickname given to the Boeing 747 aircraft. (True/False)
6. Humans have landed on Mars. (True/False)

Crossword Puzzle

Across:

1. Airships are filled with this lighter-than-air gas.

4. This aeroplane can take off and land in water.

7. A hot air balloon drifts with the ____.

8. Charles _________ was the first person to fly solo across the Atlantic in 1927 .

12. The four forces that help an aeroplane fly are - Lift, Thrust, Weight and ____.

13. This planet has been the most visited planet.

14. These objects orbit the Earth.

15. A ________ is a vehicle that travels into space.

16. Passenger seats in an airliner are placed in this part of the aeroplane.

Down:

2. Photographers use this to take aerial shots and make videos.

3. The Wright Flyer was powered by a small and light ______ engine.

5. A spacecraft without any crew onboard.

6. _______________ engineers build vehicles that fly into Outer Space.

9. Spacecrafts get their power from ________.

10. Pilots, soldiers and aviation enthusiasts use this to safely jump out from aeroplanes.

11. People sitting in the ______ control monitor rocket launches.

GLOSSARY

Aircraft	a machine capable of flying
Atmosphere	the envelope of gases surrounding the earth
Aviation	the flying or operating of aircraft
Bomber	an aircraft designed to carry and drop bombs
Cargo	goods carried on a ship, aircraft, or motor vehicle
Drift	be carried slowly by a current of air or water
Engineer	a person who designs, builds, or maintains engines, machines
Gasoline	refined petroleum used as fuel
Glide	move with a smooth, quiet continuous motion
GPS	global Positioning System, used in finding directions
Military	armed forces
Propeller	a mechanical device for pushing a boat or aircraft forward
Route	a path taken in getting from a starting point to a destination
Solo	done by one person alone
Steerable	something that can be steered
Vehicle	a thing used for transporting people or goods

ANSWERS

Page 28. 1. (d) 2. (b) 3. (a)4. (c) 5. (b)

Page 29. 1. Expands 2. Blimps 3. Glider 4. Cockpit 5. Rotor

Page 30. 1. True 2. False 3. False 4. True 5. True 6. False

Page 31.